The Definitive SEO
Local Business

Written in simple English, for the rest of us.

By David Vineyard

If after reading this book you have any questions related local SEO for your business I want you to feel free to email me and I will be more than happy to assist you and answer any questions you may have. I can be emailed at:
dvineyard@instreamsystems.com

Table of Contents

Introduction

No tricks, No secrets, just straight no frill information on how real SEO professionals get their clients sites to the first response page of Google and other search engines no matter how competitive their search keywords or phrases are.

I'm sure you remember the line from the movie Field of Dreams *"If you build it they will come"*. I can guarantee you if you build your website wrong they won't come, but if you build it right and you use what you learn in this book they will. The only thing I can't guarantee is how many visitors will come, that is up to you and the effort you put forth in your website and all the on page and off page parts that effect your placement. It will require you to develop great fresh content and provide it correctly for your sites human visitors and the search engines robot visitors.

Showing up on the first page of major search engines is critical for business success today. Getting on the first page of Google or other search engines isn't enough; you also need to strive to be above the fold. Search engine optimization which gets you there can often seem very confusing, and frustrating.

If you've tried to navigate you way through the sea of SEO advice online you may have noticed most of it is ether outdated or just plain bad advice. When people write about SEO online they often are trying to generate content to get their SEO business noticed and if they were to provide you with all the information you needed to successfully master local SEO you wouldn't need to buy services from their company.

The Definitive SEO Guide for Local Business is designed to quickly get you past the fluff and the history of SEO and dive you straight into what really works, what's required, and how to implement it to get your business, or your clients business on the first Search Engine Response Page (SERP).

Most books in this and similar subjects start by providing you the back-story or history of the subject matter, I have made a conscious decision to exclude that information as it is readily available from many sources. Instead I am focusing on how you can get the information you need so you can implement it right away and start getting more local targeted visitors to your website.

This book is designed to provide you with easy, simple to follow proven methods to get your local business on the first page of Google and other search engines; and have them above the fold in record time.

What do you mean by above the fold?

Back when newspapers were the primary source of up to date information the editor and chief of the paper always tried to come up with exciting headlines that grabbed the reader's attention so you would pick up the paper and buy it. News Papers are folded in half and displayed with the front page facing up. Above the fold was anything you could read without unfolding the news paper.

This term has carried over to the internet and specifically to websites. Above the fold of a website page is anything you can read without scrolling down the page.

Search engines are nothing more than websites themselves with the purpose of returning and displaying links to other websites that are relevant to the search term entered into a search field. Each Search engine like Google, Bing, Yahoo all have their own algorithms they have developed to return indexed information about websites.

Getting your website listed in a returned search result is determined by many factors but the basic principals are that your website has to first be indexed and then has to be relevant to the search requested by a user. The more relevant your website is to the users search the more likely your website is to be displayed on a search result and above the fold of the returned search page.

In the following chapters of this book you will learn how to get indexed, how to get on the first page, and then how to get above the fold. In many cases the process can happen in a very rapid fashion and I will show how that works as well. The chapters are laid out in order of how I always approach working with my clients and the steps I take to get their websites on the first page of search engines. So are you ready to get your website noticed online? Let's get started.

The Starting Point

I was taught at an early age that anything worth doing is worth doing well; your website is no exception. There are many things that can harm your online efforts and we are going to cover the topmost of those now. We will first look at what I call "renting versus owning".

If you are a local business owner you most likely have been contacted on numerous occasions from companies wanting to sell you SEO services. SEO companies can be categorized into several types:

1. The first type takes your existing website and performs on-page SEO modifications and your website stays on your current hosting platform.

2. The Second type of SEO Company builds a new website for you and hosts it on their servers and they own the site. This SEO type of company can and will redirect your traffic the minute you stop paying a monthly service fee.

3. The third type of SEO Company builds a new website for you and hosts it on their servers for you but you own it.

4. The forth type of SEO company charges thousands of dollars a month to do a full rework of your entire online presents. This SEO type generally works with larger websites that have thousands of daily users.

Using the four simple categories defined above the second type of SEO company is what I call renting your online presents, this is because as soon as you stop paying a monthly service fee you no longer get the benefit of the website. Furthermore any directory listings or citations can be very hard to reclaim even though your business name is attached to them. Companies like yodel™ use this business model and it is very lucrative and can be painful for a business to replace the service with their own solution.

Now that you know a little about SEO company types, it should be clear that it is better to own and not rent your business presents online.

Define Website Purpose

The first step is to determine what your website purpose is; I am sure you have a general idea.

It is important to understand your websites purpose so you can figure out what your specific target audience is. The more you can define your target audience the more you can assess your competition, what they are doing, and what you need to include in your website to be more relevant than they are.

Example website purpose:

Website XYZ.com will provide a list of business services; provide user information about why our services are needed, and what sets our services apart from our competitors.

Our Target Audience is a homeowner in need of the ABC service and is located within 50 miles of our location. Target audience will be searching for our services using a search engine and we know they want to see positive reviews from previous customers before they make a buying decision.

Armed with this information you are ready to create your workflow.

Creating Website Workflow and Structure

We used to always develop websites from front to back meaning we would develop a home page, about us, product or service pages and then a contact us page.

With all the changes in search engines and how people search you have to provide a more open architecture approach to website design allowing for more entry points and not expecting your visitors to always enter your site thru the home page.

For instance let's say you are a pest control business. You provide services related to ants, bedbugs, roaches, rodents and so forth, you will want to get search engine results under each service you provide and not just a single result linking to your home page.

Since my site visitors can enter the website thru many website pages, there are several things that need to be included to ensure a good workflow.

- Provide business identity on every page the visitor can enter the website thru so they know the business name, phone number, and address and so on.
- Provide navigation to other pages in the website so the user can get to know the business and all it has to offer.
- Provide at least two methods of contact on each page to help the user convert from a visitor to a customer. This is generally achieved by providing a phone number and a contact form of some type.

How Your Website should be coded (very important)

Every aspect of getting a business website well placed in search engine results is important, however if you get everything else right and this part wrong it will have a negative effect. Most people do not realize how important your website code structure is. From a users perspective as long as the interface is not overly complex and they can interact with the website to fulfill their need than they are relatively unaware of poor coding, however if your goal is to rank above or even close to your competitors than poor coding is not going to work.

With the combination of modifications to search engine algorithms and a change in how people search, websites are expected to provide more and more information to the search engine spider bots than ever before. This information is provided in markup code that is embedded in your websites html structure. Up until just a few years ago all you really needed to ensure was that you had the keyword Meta tag in your website header and it contained the keywords your websites page was designed to support.

Now the keyword Meta tag isn't used by most search engines at all and is only used to support smaller search engines that haven't updated their index algorithms like the larger search engines have. That is by no means saying that keywords are not important because they are, just not needed in the keyword Meta data tag.

To this day I see the lesser experienced website developer building websites and adding the keyword Meta data expecting it to get the website some sort of ranking, but in reality all they are doing is providing a simple method of letting the competition know what keywords they are targeting.

Building a website for local business has different requirements than a website built to get listed on a national or global scale. Local business websites need to let the search engines know what geolocation they are targeting. This is achieved by adding the proper Meta tags to the code that builds each page.

To add to the importance of website structure; each page the business wants to get great search engine positioning for needs to provide the important information to search engine bots as quickly as possible. This is another area where you need to understand how your visitors will read your page.

As a person I expect to see a website page provide information in a specific area of each page. I expect to see certain data in the header, navigation, body, and footer areas of a page. Search engine bots are looking for data like targeting keywords, density of keywords, location, links, and so on to score the pages relevancy, the search engine doesn't need to know where the CSS files get loaded from, how the navigation is built, or the type of 3rd party calendar control the page uses. So it has become important to order the code in a way that makes the search engines happy, while displaying the contents of the page in an order that the human users expect.

At this point we can start to develop a workflow for the website as a whole and a structure for each page.

I know the site will need a Home page even if it isn't the entry point most visitors are likely to arrive to the website thru. I will also need a Contact page, an About Us page, and since we will be providing articles about our industry the site will need a Blog page. If for example the business provides pest control services there needs to be a page for each specific service provided so we can get as many entry points and top level listings as possible.

Example: our Pest control company will provide pest control services for bedbugs, termites, ants & roaches, rodents, and silverfish. I will develop a page dedicated to our silverfish treatment service and do the same for all the other services we will provide. Our Silverfish page will be titled "silverfish-treatment Austin, TX" the description will read "Discover the professional silverfish treatments provided by XYZ extermination in Austin, TX. We have a 100% guarantee and we are price competitive".

What we have accomplished with the title and description Meta tags for the silverfish-treatment page is let the search engines know the page is related to silverfish treatments in the Austin, TX local business area. We have also let the search engines know what we want the searching public to know about our service. Below is how this page will show in a Google search.

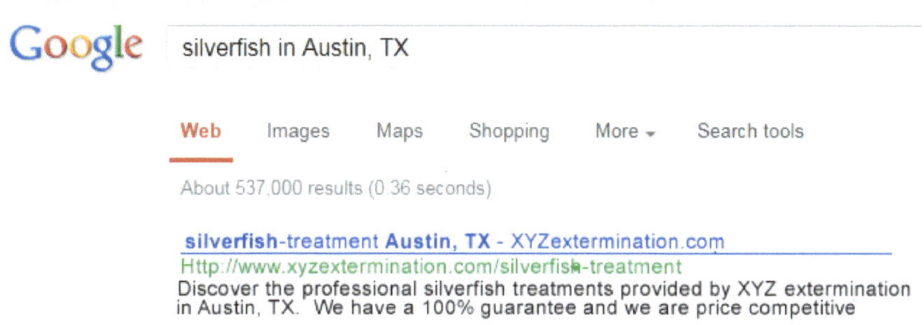

In the above example we are using silverfish-treatment as a keyword phrase. We have ensured our keyword phrase is placed in our page title and description area so the search engines will index the page properly. We will cover this topic in more depth in the Specific SEO for Local Business chapter.

Let's say we also service some surrounding towns just outside the Austin, TX area, because of the way Google and the other top search engines handle relevancy of results you will want to create what's called landing pages for those towns and include the service or keyword phrase and the town name in the title and description Meta tags for those pages.

This is very important, do not copy and paste the text on your landing pages that you use on the main service page, this will cause duplicate content and you most likely will get penalized by the search engines. Instead you can have a summarization of the service and a link to the main service page. But be sure to provide two ways for the visitor to contact you on the landing page in case they are ready to convert into a customer.

We will want to do the same for each of the services we offer. Of course in order to get great first page placement above the fold you have to ensure your page contains text that deals with the keywords used as the keyword phrase in the title and description areas. It is not only important to use the keywords on the page but you have to use them the right way as well. Your keywords need to be in the first paragraph of the page, they should be in an <h1> tag otherwise known as a header element, and used less than 10 times on the page.

Although you are trying to use your keywords on the page you never want to sacrifice the readability of the page in place of great positioning on the search engines. If you attempt to over use the keywords two things can happen, the search engines will consider you as a keyword spammer and you will be penalized and end up getting poor placement, or your text will not read normally to your human visitors and they will leave your page causing your site to have a high bounce rate. Don't worry if you do not know what a bounce rate is yet we will be covering that in the Measuring Website Results chapter a little later in the book.

Let Search Engines Know Your There

It's a beautiful thing when your business seems like it on auto pilot, your phone is ringing off the hook, your website visitors are sending you estimate request from your website, and all you have to do is focus on your work and collect the payments from happy customers.

But we are not there yet we have a great website to build and the search engines need to know we are here so they can start serving us up to the people looking for our services or products. In order to have a website we need web pages and in turn we need to know what is going on those pages. Although you know what products and services you offer; you may not be aware how people are searching for those products and services.

Start With Keyword Research

I like to start by doing a little keyword research for each page I develop. There are two types of keywords; Primes, and Niche, and then it expands to two, three, and four word phrases and so on. Primes are single keywords like books, music, painting, or electrical. These Primes are generally all but out of reach for the small business trying to capitalize on the use of search engine traffic.

But all is far from lost. The major players in internet search engine algorithm development are all working hard for your search traffic and that means they are all trying to give you what you want. So if you live in Nashville, TN and you type in electrician in the search bar your results will have local electricians listed followed by national results like Electrician - Wikipedia, the free encyclopedia, and Electricians - Bureau of Labor Statistics. This enables the local business to take full advantage of the use of Primes.

The niche types are generally much easier to get listed with and your ability to show up in search results are much more rapid when you use this type. Niche keywords also fall into the keyword phrase definition for keywords but are often overlooked by web developers and webmasters causing their use to be lower thus making it easier for you to get started with. Think of it like pushing a car along a long straight road, it can be tough to get it started but once it is moving it is much easier to keep it going.

Once your website pages get listed it is much easier for your business to get listed in the Primes, this is because the search engines now know your website is there and you are starting to build creditability with them.

There are many tools available on the market to research keywords; I recommend that at least at first you stick with the free but excellent tool available from Google. This tool is "The Google AdWords Keyword Tool". You will be required to create a free Google account, the tool is found under the Google AdWords section of Google's website. The link to access The Google AdWords Keyword Tool can be found at: https://adwords.google.com/o/KeywordTool

Using our fictitious XYZ extermination business let's take a look at how we would use the AdWords Keyword Tool to find niche keywords to use on our Silverfish page. The Prime keyword for this page is the service name silverfish. Type the Prime keyword into the Word or phrase text field and select the Search button. We could drill down further by using the website or category fields but we are going to keep it simple for now.

Below is an example of the AdWords Tool

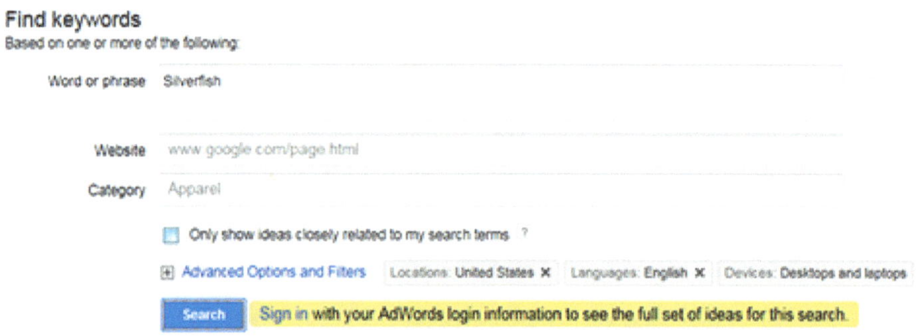

Find keywords
Based on one or more of the following:
Word or phrase Silverfish
Website www.google.com/page.html
Category Apparel
Only show ideas closely related to my search terms
Advanced Options and Filters Locations: United States Languages: English Devices: Desktops and laptops
Search Sign in with your AdWords login information to see the full set of ideas for this search.

In a matter of seconds the tool returns a list of keywords that represent how people looking for Silverfish information or services searched on Google. This is important for several reasons; for one thing it tells you exactly what word combinations you can expect your site visitors to use when they search for your products or services. Another important result is it shows you how many local searches you can expect to be performed each month in your business area. You will also see the level of difficulty you can expect to encounter if you decide to use that keyword or phrase.

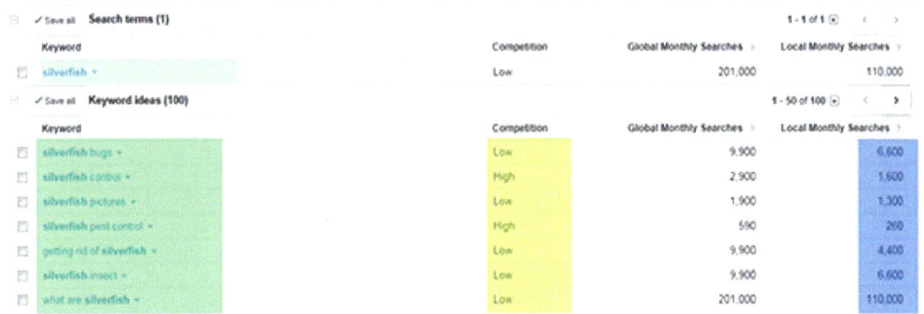

✓ Save all Search terms (1) — 1 - 1 of 1

Keyword	Competition	Global Monthly Searches	Local Monthly Searches
silverfish	Low	201,000	110,000

✓ Save all Keyword ideas (100) — 1 - 50 of 100

Keyword	Competition	Global Monthly Searches	Local Monthly Searches
silverfish bugs	Low	9,900	6,600
silverfish control	High	2,900	1,600
silverfish pictures	Low	1,900	1,300
silverfish pest control	High	590	260
getting rid of silverfish	Low	9,900	4,400
silverfish insect	Low	9,900	6,600
what are silverfish	Low	201,000	110,000

Notice the highlighted columns, The Green or first column is the returned keywords. The first is our seed keyword or our Prime Followed by Niche keywords. The Niche keywords have two or more words together making a Niche phrase.

The Yellow or second column shows the level of competition from Low to High. And the last or blue column shows you the average monthly local searches for each keyword or niche phrase.

It can seem a bit difficult at first to decipher the data provided, for example notice the competition level of the Prime keyword is showing as Low. Then notice the number of Local monthly searches is 110,000. When you realize that if all sites related to silverfish only used the Prime keyword it would be hard for a search engine or human to understand if the website was about how to treat silverfish bites, or about how our service can treat a silverfish infestation.

Although the competition level is low you must take into consideration the amount of traffic involved as well. It's allot like if you entered into a competition to win $10,000 and all you had to do was drink a can of soda and hand the empty can to someone judging the competition, sounds easy right? Well it would be except in this case there are 109,999 others doing the same thing and you have to get pass them in order to reach the person judging the competition and hand them your empty can so now it isn't as easy as it first seemed.

Now take a look at the keyword phrase *"silverfish pest control"*, the competition level is high but there are only 260 monthly local searches. It wouldn't be worth attempting to position our business in a high competition keyword phrase when only 260 people are performing searches using those keywords a month.

The list does show a great diamond in the rough and it will make for a good niche phrase to use. Look again at the results and you will see "silverfish insect" and it has a low competition level with a reasonable number of people searching for it locally each month. This is our target keyword phrase and it fits well with our service. Now I can design a page for silverfish and have a title and description containing *"silverfish insect"* included and I can have a section on the page that talk about Behavior, Diet & Habits of Silverfish and it could read something like:

[Behavior, Diet & Habits

Silverfish feed on carbohydrates, particularly sugars and starches. Cellulose, shampoos, glue in books, linen, silk and dead insects may be food sources, have been found in unopened food packages.]

You should try to find two or three Niche keyword phrases to use per service page to broaden your abilities to be relevant on as many searches as possible.

So we have covered how to find our niche keyword phrases to use on our web page but we need to ensure the search engine bots index our web page and to make sure they do that the first thing we need to do is let them they know they have our permission.

Robot.txt

Web Robots or webBots also called spiders and crawlers are unmanned applications or scripts used by Google and other search engines to automate the process of navigating thru websites to learn how they should be indexed. The Robot.txt file is a plain text file located in the root directory of the website to provide instructions to the webBots that visit the website. When a webBot visits a website it first looks for a robot.txt file for instructions on how to process a website. The robot.txt file will tell the webBot what pages to look at and can omit pages the webmaster does not want to be indexed. Below is an example of a robot.txt file:

User-agent:*

Disallow:

This robot.txt file tells the webBot that all webBots are allowed and that all paged can be indexed. To disallow all webBots from indexing the website you would use: Disallow:/

To disallow webBots from indexing a specific folder use: disallow: /temp/ or /reports/.

To disallow webBots from indexing a specific page use: disallow: / reports/reports.html.

To exclude a specific webBot use:

User-agent: BotName

Disallow: /

If you do not create a robot.txt file it acts the same as allowing full indexing of the site. However I recommend you create a robot.txt file and add your sitemap location in it so your site gets properly indexed.

User-agent:*

Disallow:

Sitemap: http://www.YourWebsiteAddress.com/sitemap.xml

Sitemap.xml

Sitemaps tell search engines about the pages of your website that can be crawled for indexing. A sitehmap will contain important information for each available page including how often the page content is updated and how relevant the page is in relation to other pages in the site.

A sitemap.xml file must be properly encoded using UTF-8 encoding. The formation of the sitemap requires special tags in proper order to be read by the search engine below is an example of a sitemap:

<?xml version="1.0" encoding="UTF-8"?>

<urlset xmlns=http://www.sitemaps.org/schemas/sitemap/0.9>

<url>

<loc>http://www.yourwebsite.com/index.html</loc>

<lastmod>2013-08-12</lastmod>

<changefreq>monthly</changefreq>

<priority>0.8</priority>

</url>

</urlset>

The below table shows both the required and optional tags in XML site maps.

Site Map Tags in XML

Tag	**Required or Optional**	**Explanation**
<urlset>	Required	Encapsulates the file and references the current protocol standard.
<url>	Required	Parent tag for each URL entry. The remaining tags are children of this tag.
<loc>	Required	URL of the page. This URL must begin with the protocol (such as http) and end with a trailing slash, if your Web server requires it. This value must be less than 2048 characters.
<lastmod>	Optional	The date of last modification of the file. This date should be in W3C Datetime format. This format allows you to omit the time portion, if desired, and use the YYYY-MM-DD format.
<changefreq>	Optional	How frequently the page is likely to change. This value provides general information to search engines and may not correlate exactly to how often they crawl the page.
<priority>	Optional	The priority of this URL relative to other URLs on your site. Valid values range from 0.0 to 1.0. This value has no effect on your pages compared to pages on other sites and only lets the search engines know which of your pages you deem most important so that they can order the crawl of your pages in the way you prefer. The default priority of a page is 0.5. You should set your landingpages at a higher priority and non-landing pages at a lower one.

A great resource for learning more about sitemap can be found on the Google website at: https://support.google.com/webmasters/answer/183668?hl=en#2

Submitting your site to Search Engines

The web is full of companies willing to submit your website to a long list of search engines and my advice is to ignore tempting offers and do it yourself. Each search engine has made it clear they prefer you submit your website manually yourself than to have a third party company do it especially if they use software to mass submit.

Where to submit?

You should at minimum submit your site to Google, Yahoo, and Bing search engines. Site submittal for each search engine is a little different but for the most part is very straight forward.

Search Engine	**URL**
Google	http://www.google.com/submityourcontent/business-owner/#
Yahoo	http://search.yahoo.com/info/submit.html
Bing	http://www.bing.com/toolbox/submit-site-url

Google's message to webmasters on their webmaster Tools site submittal page is:

"Google adds new sites to our index, and updates existing ones, every time we crawl the web. If you have a new URL, tell us about it here. We don't add all submitted URLs to our index, and we can't make predictions or guarantees about when or if submitted URLs will appear in our index."

My experience with Google has been that they add local business websites to their index within 1-4 weeks of being submitted. If you don't see your sites indexed within 4-weeks then simply resubmit it. You can verify if your website has been indexed by searching for your website name i.e. "*mywebsitename*" on each search engine you submitted your site to.

Importance of Links & How to Get Them

The topic of links is a complete book in itself and my goal here is to give you the information you need to get on the first page of Google and other search engines and stay there. For this reason I will limit the discussion of links to only what you need to know to become successful in your goal without falling into the bad-link traps.

The most talked about links are links from other websites to your website otherwise known as backlinks. It is so important to get the right backlinks to the point that it is better to not have any backlinks than to have the wrong backlinks. A bad backlink is from a website known by the search engines to have a bad reputation. The real fact is you do not have to have any backlinks to get on the first page of Google or other search engines but you won't get there with one or two keywords. Without positive backlinks it would require you to use five or more keywords known as a keyword phrase to get on the first page of Google. You might be thinking that doesn't sound too bad; however you have to take into consideration how people use search engines and what they type in as a search term.

Most people will type the name of what they are looking for, or one to three words describing what they are searching for, typically not a sentence of what they are searching for. An example would be a person searching for a house painter in Miami Florida. The person would type in "House Painter, Home Painter, or Best Painting Company"; they typically would not type in "House Painter in Miami, FL on Spring Street". The difference is how competitive the keywords are going to be. The keywords "House Painter" will be very competitive in any area because that search term encompasses all house painters in the area. The keyword phrase "House Painter in Miami, Fl on Spring Street" is not going to be competitive because it will most likely only represent one or two companies and the search volume will be very low.

To overcome high competition for keywords your site has to be more relevant that your competition and it helps to have more citations or backlinks than your competition. A higher volume of citations or backlinks tells the search engine your website is popular and search engines want to provide their users with the best results for each search.

What to Avoid

Many companies sprouted up almost overnight promising hundreds if not thousands of backlinks to your website for $50.00 or less. These companies mostly run scripts and other automated software that blindly submit your website information to directories and blog sites. Many sites used for this purpose do not have a very good reputation with the search engines and can cause your site to gain a bad reputation. Backlinks from websites that are not related to the main content on your website do very little to help your website gain ground. In other words if your business sales paint and painting supplies it does little to no good to have a backlink from a lawn service website, or from a blog post about diabetes.

Different Types of Links

Links or backlinks for local business will generally come from citations, directories, and other businesses your company does business with. Local businesses use citations to let people and search engines know they are local to a given area. Citations and backlinks are referred to as off site SEO meaning it is not part of the SEO you do on your website but it is very important to your websites overall SEO process. We will learn where to get our citations from later in the “Specific SEO for Local Business” chapter, for now let’s get a better understanding of what a citation is.

An example would be an automotive company looking to increase awareness of their business would create citations on sites like Yelp, Citysearch, and Google plus. These citations help prove you are local to an area and help create new local traffic to your website. Citations are also a great way to get on Google fast.

Example, say we search for “automotive shop” in Austin, Tx. Notice the results brought back by Google, the first three organic results are all from Yelp.

Google search for automotive shop, Austin,Tx

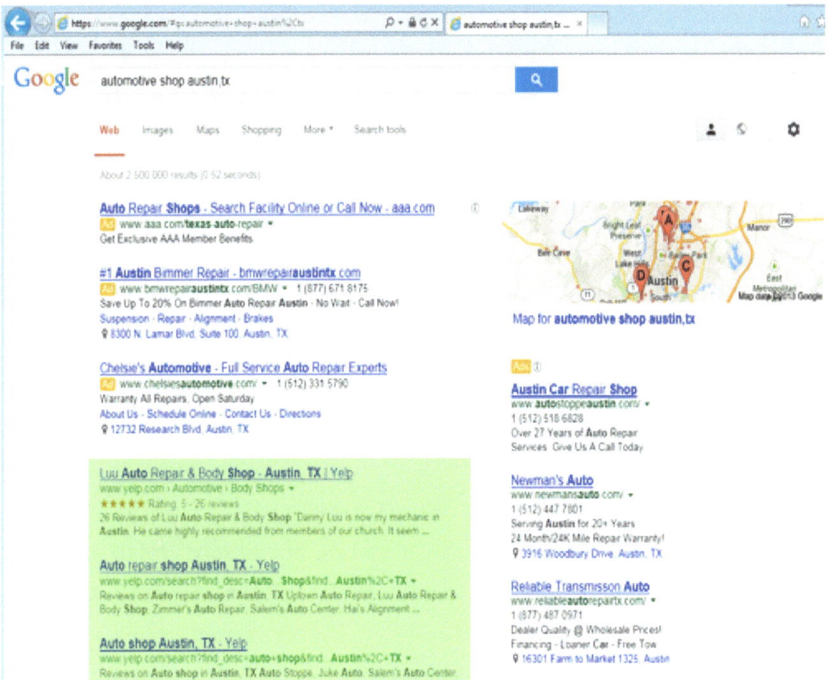

The main difference between a backlink and a citation is that citations provide user interaction and allow users to provide feedback from their experience with your company in the form of reviews. Once you have your citations setup you should ask every customer to fill out a review, try giving them a discount for a positive review. The positive reviews will pay off in more new business.

Arboretum, Great Hills
4918 Hamilton Rd
Austin, TX 78759
(512) 343-7711

Austin **Auto** Techs was a great find! I have been there 3 times and will continue to go to their **shop** for 3 big reasons: -The mechanics at **Auto** Techs straight talk you and explain your problems

The best advertisement you can ever do as a small local business is to get your customers to speak positively about the experience they had doing business with you. The power of a satisfied customer has started a new business model for several companies like AngiesList, and HomeAdvisor that take advantage of this importance and charge customers for access to these lists like at AngiesList or charge the company for a "Hot lead" like at HomeAdvisor.

How Many Links or Citations Do You Need?

This is one of the most asked questions and one of the most mislead when answered. The short answer is that you can at times get away without having any, however to compete you need as many as you can get. If you post a blog and your trying to become the most relevant for the search phrase like " How to become the most relevant in 2014" you can create a post with that exact title and use the phrase several times in the post. You can put the post in a sub folder using the same word phrase and use the word phrase as H1 and H2 tags. For a local response on a search this would most likely be more than enough to get on the first page in at least the lower part of the page if not better.

It has been my experience that the best answer comes from asking that question for every page, post, video or search keyword you target. There are several tools you can use to help come up with a great answer, I use an application named Ultimate Niche Finder when searching for keywords to target, however there are many applications you can find and use. Below is a screen shot of a search on the keywords auto repair I ran in Ultimate Niche Finder. The column [Top Links] shows how many incoming links the top website has for that keyword phrase, and the next column shows how difficult it is to gain the top spot for that keyword.

Keyword	Avg. Monthly	CPC	Competition	Results	Top Links	Difficulty
auto repair [801 expanded]	40500	6.81	0.93	140,000,000	1	Moderate
auto repair estimates	1900	6.24	0.95	8,750,000	7,797	Hard
auto repair shops	18100	8.17	0.98	72,500,000	0	Moderate
auto repair shop	3600	7.87	0.88	115,000,000	0	Moderate
auto repair estimate	480	7.51	0.91	11,900,000	7,797	Hard

There are several great pieces of information in the above graphic that can help positively impact your SEO efforts. First the results show the average number of times a month that exact keyword phrase is searched on in a Google search. Next it shows how many links the top websites using that search phrase have coming into that page. Another important column is showing how difficult it is to become a top page for that keyword phrase.

What you will want to do is find keyword phrases that match your content, have a large number of monthly searches with the lowest level of difficulty and require the lowest number of inbound links.

So there is the true answer, there is not a single number of citations or inbound links you need, it is based on competition for a given keyword or keyword phrase. Your job will be to find the best keywords and phrases you can compete for in your local area that match the content on your page, post, or video.

How to Get Citations and Backlinks

Citations are important to local business placement on search engines; they are great at evening the playing field between a small local business and a large national company with a marketing budget. Search engines like Google display relevant results that contain a mixture of local and national brands with each page result. In the chapter Specific SEO for Local Business we will detail exactly how to develop citations and other backlinks but for now it is important to understand how to generate a list of citations and backlinks that will be important for your specific business to have. Readers of this book are comprised of a very wide verity of businesses and cover many different products and services. The citations and links that are important for a shoe repair shop are not always the same as those needed for an auto repair shop or pest control company. There will be some citations and links that span across all local businesses however and there are many specific to the business your company is in.

The best way to start is with a list of citations that cross all businesses in the local market. There are hundreds of citations your business can use however to start we will focus on the top citations used by all the top search engines.

List of Citations:

- Yelp
- Yellow pages
- Citysearch
- Yahoo Local
- Superpages
- Facebook
- youTube
- Manta

- City Data
- BBB
- Google Plus

As state above, there are hundreds of citation sites. Don't feel like you have to have all of them and although there are companies available to automate this process do not use a service to populate them for you. I assure you the best results come from you manually inputting in your information. Each citation site is simple to use and it only takes a few minutes to complete each entry.

Note: It is very important you provide the same address, phone number, email address, website address and company name for each citation site so they properly link up to your business.

List of Backlinks:

To confirm to the latest changes Google has made to their search index algorithm over the past few years I generally will not list backlink sites, instead you will want to replace backlink sites with directories and obtain backlinks from reliable sources in your businesses field of expertise.

Google Places
Facebook
LinkedIn
Yellowpages.com
Yelp
Local.com
WhitePages.com
Manta
SuperPages
CitySearch

Patch
City-Data
MerchantCircle
Yellowbook.com
Yahoo Local
Mapquest
Topix
DexKnows
Yellow.com
BBB.org
HomeAdvisor
Angieslist
AreaConnect
Foursquare
AmericanTowns

After looking thru both the citation and directories lists you may have noticed some sites like Citysearch, BBB, Yahoo Local, and more are in both lists. Some sites have multiple purposes and therefore fulfill both the needs of a citation and a directory.

As with the citations it is not necessary to be listed in all the directories, at least not right away. Pick a handful to get started and add more as you have time. The lists above are not complete lists but they are the top most in both citation and business directory sites. Later in the Specific SEO for Local Business chapter we will walk you step by step thru creating a citation and a directory listing.

Social Media & Video

Social Media

I'm sure you know the power of social media and how quickly news can spread, but for a local business it is rare that you will have thousands of followers and friends that will see your post and updates. It is still important to maintain a positive presence on social media and it will prove to be useful to generate new business as well.

The best approach to social media is to minimize the number of social sites you use for your business and follow the 8 to 1 ratio rule. Limiting the number of social sites you use will enable you to maintain a constant dialog without becoming overwhelmed with the daily tasks. For most local businesses today the top two social sites will be Facebook and Twitter.

As a local business with a social presence it becomes your responsibility to engage your followers and friends by providing relevant content. Relevant content means you should direct your posts to the proper subject matter, so if you are an automotive shop your topics should always be about the automotive field and not politics or other topics that could minimize your friends and followers thoughts of the business.

It is very important to realize that if you want to gain friends and followers and keep them you need to provide them a reason to stick around. Your post should be informative like how to get more miles out of a set of tires, or how to check fluid levels in a car. As mentioned above there is a 8 to 1 rule for businesses in social media, that rule is for every 8 informative post you can create 1 self serving post like an ad or a coupon for discounted service.

Use social media to create positive backlinks to your website by writing articles and posting a link to them on each social media account you have. An example would be to create a step-by-step article on how to check the oil in a car. After you have written the article create a post like this:

Facebook post –

Save Money – Learn how to change the oil in your car. A great step-by-step guide.

This step by step guide makes it easy to change the oil and oil filter in your own Car saving you money each time you do it yourself.

http://www.yourwebsiteaddress.com/oil_change/oilchange_article.html

Brought to you by XYZ Automotive

http:// www.yourwebsiteaddress.com

Twitter post –

Save Money – Learn how to change the oil in your car. A great step-by-step guide.
http://www.yourwebsiteaddress.com/oil_change/oilchange_article.html

Video

Two main reasons video is so important to the overall SEO for your website are (1) video makes for great website content and (2) YouTube will get you on the front page of Google in hours not weeks or months. Of course your video needs to be as professional as possible and the meta data is as important as the video its self. You may not realize it but Google is the *largest* search engine in the world, and YouTube is the *second-largest* search engine in the world. Both are owned by Google and feed each other content that people search for and want to see. The way video is going to help is by providing the right meta data for the content. The meta data is going to tell YouTube how to index your video content.

The Key things to include for Meta data are:

Title:

Make your title compelling – this is your video's headline. Titles and thumbnails are often the primary elements driving viewers' to click on your video. When defining your title ask yourself If you searched for a video of the same content type and saw your title would you click on it?

Title Key thoughts:

- Always represent your content accurately.
- Offer keywords first, branding at the end.
- Create a title that reinforces the thumbnail (a thumbnail is a still frame from your video)- make sure that together they tell a cohesive story.
- If your video will cover a single part of a continuous video series make sure to number what video the current one is and reflect it in your title

Tags

Tags are the keywords that will help people find your videos. Create a group of tags for your YouTube channel that can be applied to all the videos you publish. If you are an Automotive shop you should include tags like "Automotive, Auto Repair, Car Repair, Auto repair Videos, Mechanic shop". Use enough tags to thoroughly and accurately describe the video you publish and ensure to use keywords in your title.

Description

The Video description is very important and is the first thing potential viewers will see of your video. Only the first few sentences of your description will appear in search results or above the fold on a video page

– so make them count. A video description should accurately describe your video in one or two concise sentences. A video description can Link to sites, videos, channels or users referenced in your video.

There are many free resources available online that can teach you how to create great video to publish on your YouTube channel.

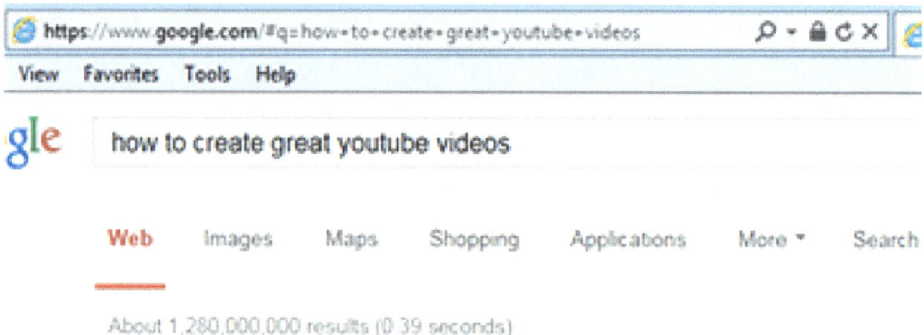

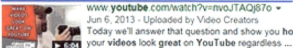

3 Ways to Make Yourself Famous on YouTube - wikiHow
www.wikihow.com › ... › YouTube
Jump to Making Great Videos - Offer something great to your audience. If you look through the most popular YouTube videos, you'll see that each one ...

How To Make Videos Look Great on YouTube - YouTube

www.youtube.com/watch?v=nwoJTAQj87o
Jun 6, 2013 - Uploaded by Video Creators
Today we'll answer that question and show you how to make your videos look great on YouTube regardless ...

How to create great videos about your business - YouTube

www.youtube.com/watch?v=3-fcr5gHO1w
Oct 14, 2011 - Uploaded by helloGoogle
Watch more videos at http://www.youtube.com/hellogoogle?x=youtube Bing Chen, YouTube Creator ...

How to create a great video commercial - YouTube

www.youtube.com/watch?v=193eNBHaGDg
Mar 20, 2013 - Uploaded by Matthew Ferrara
Matthew Ferrara offers three tips to real estate professionals on how to create great video commercials.

How to Create Great Videos - Nine Rules for Creating ... - YouTube

www.youtube.com/watch?v=C7L0-3Lq0WA
Apr 9, 2012 - Uploaded by NovoMediaUSA
http://www.novomediausa.com Creating video doesn't have to be difficult, but there are rules that will help ...

How to Make GREAT YouTube Videos EASILY! - YouTube
www.youtube.com/watch?v=n6aK-ISYHxo

With a simple search you can gain all the information you need to get started and I have no doubt you will become a pro in no time. In reality your first few videos may not have a lot of views but they go a long way in letting the key search engines know your business and website exists so take as much advantage of this free forum as often as possible.

Specific SEO for Local Business

Each search engine response page has three primary areas your website can appear at. The first is the Ad's section, this section is for adWords users and you will pay a cost per click to be in this area. The second is the Map section, and the Third is the organic section. As a local business you will strive to get placed in both the Maps and organic sections of the first page as these areas do not cost you money. For select businesses like restaurants there is a forth section known as the carousel and is displayed at the top of the search page.

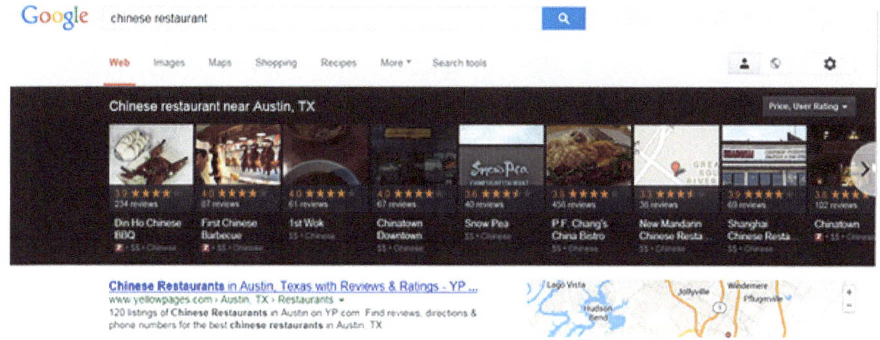

You will notice that the above search returned Chinese restaurants near Austin, TX although I simply typed in the keywords chinese restaurant. This is because Google is using Geo Location to determine I am performing a search on a device that is in or near the Austin, TX area, this helps Google return results more relevant than a list of restaurants in another city.

In this chapter we will walk you step by step thru each of the important steps needed to create a powerful SEO presence for your business. First we will show you why local SEO is different from a national SEO effort. Next we will gain an understanding of the factors in a local search and how they impact you as a local business. Then we will add citations and directories for our local SEO efforts as well as learn how to build user reviews. We have a lot to cover in this chapter so let's get started.

Why Local SEO is Different

Local SEO is designed to promote your business to local customers, by reaching them right at the moment they are searching for a solution your business provides. Unlike a search for something like *"how the earth was formed"* a local search for a product or service uses geographical location of the user to provide results. Almost 60% of users rely on search engines to find businesses, so it is crucial they can find your business when they perform a search. I can't imagine having a company and expect to become successful if I eliminate 60% of my potential business by not being found on a search result.

While general principles of local SEO are the same as optimizing any other page, there are certain differences you will want to focus on:

1. How often has your website been cited on authority sites?
2. How many reviews have your customers shared?
3. How positive are the reviews from your past customers?

Positive feedback can have a major impact on your local search rankings. That's why asking your clients to provide positive reviews is so important.

Displaying a physical address will help your business rank higher for searches originating in the same geographical area, and having citations and business directory listings showing your business is well established in the area will help even more.

Here are some important tips that will help your local business website rank higher through local SEO:

1. Get listed on Google Places. Claim your business listing, and add photos, videos and maps that make it easier for new clients to find your business.
2. Ensure wider distribution of this information through services like Yext. Each listing serves as a 'citation', which collectively boosts your ranking.
3. Social profiles add value to your local search listing, so strive to generate buzz on social networks.
4. Optimize your website for on-site factors. Choose the right terms to target.
5. Build links with anchor text that includes your target city/state name, or even zip codes.
6. Use schema local markup that informs search engines that your website is targeting audiences in a specific location.
7. Be proactive about getting positive reviews from satisfied clients. This can make a big difference in your search engine rankings.
8. Add a KML (keyhole markup language) file to your website.

I know if you are not a professional website developer this can sound a bit overwhelming but don't be discouraged just yet; we are going to walk thru all the important steps to help make you successful in your local SEO efforts.

First we will focus on how your website is developed and the easiest way to do this is to start on the home page. Over the past several years website development has changed as well as how users enter your website. It used to be that users would enter your website thru your home page and navigate from there. The reality is that users can enter thru any of your pages and must be able to navigate from any page they visit to any other area of your website. I generally prefer to develop the home page and all required navigation and reuse the navigation throughout the rest of the website.

When developing with SEO in mind you want to provide all the important SEO elements as early in the html document as possible. For example the navigation may be provided at the top of the page but it can and should be coded lower in the document than meta data and the page content.

What are Local Search Factors?

Local search factors refer to positive and negative ranking factors that directly affect your businesses websites ranking and position on result pages. There are hundreds of factors that can affect your website however we are going to focus on the ones that will affect your website the most. For a complete breakdown of factors and further reading visit http://moz.com/local-search-ranking-factors to gain a higher insight into factors. For the purpose of this book we will concentrate on the following:

Positive Ranking Factors

Positive factors are applied to your business website, citations, directory listings, social media accounts, and reviews. I have listed to most relevant positive factors that will affect your website SEO the most.

1 Proper Category Associations

2 Physical Address in City of Search

3 Consistency of Structured Citations

4 Quality/Authority of Structured Citations

5 HTML NAP Matching Place Page NAP NAP = Name, Address, Phone

6 Quantity of Structured Citations (IYPs, Data Aggregators)

7 Domain Authority of Website

8 Individually Owner-verified Local Plus Page

9 City, State in Places Landing Page Title

10 Proximity of Address to Centroid

11 Quality/Authority of Inbound Links to Domain

12 Quantity of Native Google Places Reviews (w/text)

13 Product / Service Keyword in Business Title

14 Quantity of Citations from Locally-Relevant Domains

15 Proximity of Physical Location to the Point of Search\n(Searcher-Business Distance)

16 Quantity of Citations from Industry-Relevant Domains

17 Local Area Code on Local Plus Page

18 City, State in Most/All Website Title Tags

The point is not that you have all of the above covered right from the start but that you do a good job of covering as much as you can. Below when we develop the websites html layout we will cover several of the factors. When we add citations we will cover a few more of them, and we will cover a few more when we start to get customers to create reviews.

Negative Ranking Factors

As you would expect negative factors will affect your business websites SEO efforts in a negative way and you should do everything possible avoid them.

1 Listing detected at false business location

2 Keyword stuffing in business name

3 Mis-match NAP / Tracking Phone Numbers Across Data Ecosystem

4 Incorrect business category

5 Presence of Multiple Place Pages with Same/Similar Business Title and Address

6 Mis-match NAP / Tracking Phone Number on Places Landing Page

7 Mis-match Address on Places Landing Page

8 Reports of Violations on your place page

9 Presence of malware on site

10 Absence of Crawlable NAP on Website

11 Presence of Multiple Place Pages with Same Phone Number

12 Including Location Keyword in Categories

13 Absence of Crawlable NAP on Places Landing Page

14 Incorrectly placing your map marker

15 Presence of Multiple Categories in Same Input Field

16 Association of Google Places account with other suppressed listings

17 Address includes suite number similar to UPS Mail Store addresses

18 Keyword/city stuffed Place page descriptions

19 Non-Compliant Categories (those that do not fit

20 Listing 800 Number as Only Phone Number on Place Page

21 Presence of Multiple Crawlable NAP on Places Landing Page

22 Keyword-Stuffing in Title Tag of Places Landing Page

23 Choosing to Hide Place Page Address

Like with the positive factors I have listed only some of the negative factors however the above negative factors will affect your efforts the most. While looking over the list you should notice a lot of them are easily avoided by paying close attention you entering in your business information on your business website and on citation and directory sites.

A key take away from the above is to simply do the right things the right way and your business website will have a great starting point that will help lead to SEO success.

Develop the sites HTML layout

An important starting point is your business websites HTML layout. How well you develop your html tags, and the order you position the tags are vital to your sites SEO success. It is important to present all your SEO tags and Meta data as close to the top of the document as you can. Items like navigation will display at the top of the page but should be defined in the lower section of the document.

As stated earlier in this book your website has two types of users and you need to develop the website to fill the needs of both. The first user type is the search engine bots that look at your website page by page to determine how each page should be indexed if at all. The second user type is the human user that visits your website to determine if your company can and should fill their need for a product or service. When developing a website I generally will start by filling the need of the first user type primarily because it will be the first user to visit my website but also it creates the building blocks the rest of the website will be built on.

While filling the need of the first user I develop my HTML document by placing all the SEO specific tags as top most in the document as possible. The SEO tags include Title, Description, Logo, H1, H2, H3, Address, Tel, Author, and any tags that hold the content for the page. I will place footer, navigation, styling, useful links, and any other tags or content specific to the second user lower in the HTML document. The first user the search engine bots do not care what our website looks like, how wonderful our graphics are, or what font we use, but they do care about how our document is formatted and what our HTML tags tell them about our web page. The first user is looking for information about where we are, what we are about, what we offer, and how relevant we are to the search keywords we are targeting.

If you have developed a website before you most likely used the keyword Meta tag. Google and other search engines have moved away from using this tag as part of the criteria of determining the target keywords for a web page, instead they look at what the key topic is as defined in the title, h1 & h2 tags, as well as the content available on the page. I do not recommend using the keyword Meta tag unless you just want to inform your competition of what your keyword targets are.

Below is an example of a simple well formatted HTML document. For now this document is developed to fulfill the needs of the first user, we can later fulfill the needs of the second user.

Custom Auto Repair Homepage

Schedule Service Request a Quote Schedule Service Order Parts Roadside Assistance Contact Us

Auto Repair > Custom Auto Repair

Auto Repair

At Custom Auto Repair we have provided Auto Repair services in the Austin, TX area since 1987 and have gained hundreds of satisfied customers that come back for service anytime they have a need. We treat our customers like an extension of our family and we always provide the highest quality parts and service. Our goal is to always get you in and out of our service center as quickly as possible at the lowest cost to our customers.

Auto Repair Services

All of our **Auto Repair Services** are covered by a 100% satisfaction guarantee for 90-days and our parts are warranted for a full year.

Custom Auto Repair Roadside Assistance Program

Custom Auto Repair strives to be a special Auto Repair shop. Our Roadside Assistance Program protects you should you find yourself in need of assistance while on the road, at home, or at the office. Simply call us and we will pick you and your automobile up and get you back on the road as quickly as possible.

Custom Auto Repair
100 1st street
Austin, TX 78704
PH:(512)555-1212 | Fax:(512)555-1212
Email:info@ourwebsite.com

© Copyright 2014 Custom Auto Repair

Starting that the top left of the page we have defined the logo.

Down one line and to the right of the page we have our navigation menu. We will look at where the navigation is defined in our HTML document in a minute, for now just notice it appears at the top of the web page.

Next we have our breadcrumbs on the third line to the left of the page. If you are not familiar with breadcrumbs they show our website users where they are in terms of the layout of the website.

Next we have our H1 tag displaying our keyword phrase "Auto repair". Also note not shown in the above image; our page title contains our keyword phrase as well and we will look at that in the document code in a minute.

Below our H1 tag we have some page content and below that we have our H2 tag also containing our keyword phrase followed by more page content.

Next we have our H3 tag again containing our keyword phrase followed by more page content.

Finally we have our footer that contains our address tag, tel tag, email tag and copyright tag.

Up to this point our web page is not very visually appealing but it provides our web pages first user "the search engine bots" a lot of great information to work with. Let's take a look at the HTML markup code that builds this page.

```
<!DOCTYPE html>
<html lang="en">

<head>
<meta http-equiv="Content-Type" content="text/html; charset=utf-8" />
<title>Auto Repair - Custom Auto Repair Austin, TX</title>
<meta name="description" content="Full service Auto Repair on all make and models of domestic and import cars, trucks, vans,
<link rel="stylesheet" href="style.css" type="text/css" />
</head>

<body>
<div id="body">
<span class="logo"><a href="/">Custom Auto Repair Homepage</a></span><br />
<div id="bodyDiv">
  <div id="service">
    <h1>Auto Repair</h1>
    <p>At Custom Auto Repair we have provided Auto Repair services in the Austin, TX area since 1987 and have gained hundrec

    <h2>Auto Repair Services</h2>
    <p>All of our <strong>Auto Repair Services</strong> are covered by a 100% satisfaction guarantee for 90-days and our par

      <h3>Custom Auto Repair Roadside Assistance Program</h3>
        <p>Custom Auto Repair strives to be a special Auto Repair shop. Our Roadside Assistance Program protects you should
    </div>

<div class="footer">
<span class ="location">
<address>
        <br><strong>Custom Auto Repair</strong>
        <br>100 1st street
        <br>Austin, TX 78704
        <br>PH:<a href="tel:(512)555-1212"">(512)555-1212</a>| | Fax:(512)555-1212
        <br>Email:<a href="mailto:info@ourwebsite.com">info@ourwebsite.com</a>
</address>
</span>
<br /><br />
  <span class="copyright">&copy Copyright 2014 <a href="http://www.ourwebsite.com/">Custom Auto Repair</a></span>
   </div>
  </div>


<ul id="navigation">
<li><a href="http://www.ourwebsite.com/AutoRepair/service">Schedule Service</a></li>
    <li><a href="http://www.ourwebsite.com/AutoRepair/quote">Request a Quote</a></li>
    <li><a href="http://www.ourwebsite.com/AutoRepair/schedule">Schedule Service</a></li>
    <li><a href="http://www.ourwebsite.com/AutoRepair/order">Order Parts</a></li>
    <li><a href="http://www.ourwebsite.com/AutoRepair/roadside">Roadside Assistance</a></li>
    <li><a href="http://www.ourwebsite.com/AutoRepair/contact">Contact Us</a></li>
  </ul>

  <ul id="breadcrumb">
    <li><a href="/Auto Repair/">Auto Repair</a></li>
    <li>></li>
    <li>Custom Auto Repair</li>
  </ul>

  </div>
</body>
</html>
```

Let's look at each section of this HTML document. The first section is the head tag.

```
<head>
<meta http-equiv="Content-Type" content="text/html; charset=utf-8" />
<title>Auto Repair - Custom Auto Repair Austin, TX</title>
<meta name="description" content="Full service Auto Repair on all make and models of domestic and import cars, trucks, vans,
<link rel="stylesheet" href="style.css" type="text/css" />
</head>
```

The head tag contains our Meta tags like description and eventually will hold other Meta data like Author, and canonical discussed later in this chapter. It also holds our page title tag and a style sheet we need to reference. In the above our title tag makes use of our keyword phrase and tells our users we are located in the Austin, TX area. The description Meta tag provides a readable description of our business, what we do, and the type of content found on the web page. The stylesheet holds out CSS data that will provide instructions about how to format our HTML document.

The next section of our HTML document is the body tag.

```
<body>
<div id="body">
<span class="logo"><a href="/">Custom Auto Repair Homepage</a></span><br />
<div id="bodyDiv">
```

The body tag holds our page content and defines our page height and width by the body tags class. The span tag using the logo class holds a link to our page and will eventually contain our company logo graphic.

The next code section is the service tag. It holds several other tags important to our on page SEO.

```
<div id="service">
  <h1>Auto Repair</h1>
  <p>At Custom Auto Repair we have provided Auto Repair services in the Austin, TX area since 1987 and have gained hundre

  <h2>Auto Repair Services</h2>
  <p>All of our <strong>Auto Repair Services</strong> are covered by a 100% satisfaction guarantee for 90-days and our par

    <h3>Custom Auto Repair Roadside Assistance Program</h3>
      <p>Custom Auto Repair strives to be a special Auto Repair shop. Our Roadside Assistance Program protects you should
  </div>
```

The H1 tag makes use of our keyword phrase we are targeting "Auto Repair". Below the H1 tag is a P tag that holds a paragraph of page content specific to the H1 tag.

Below the H1 tags P tag is the H2 tag and the P tag specific to the H2 tag. The H2 tag also makes use of our keyword phrase we are targeting. The same holds true for the H3 tag below the H2 tags P tag.

Each of the P tags hold content that is not only specific to each header tag but also makes use of the Keyword phrase.

It is important that we try to use our keyword phrase throughout our page content but it should not be forced meaning the use of the keyword phrase must read normally and make sense. The page content is not only important to the first user but is very important to the second user "the human user" in their decision making process.

The next section holds our footer content. Our footer defines the visible end of our HTML page for our second user as well as more SEO content for our first user.

```
<div class="footer">
<span class ="location">
<address>
        <br><strong>Custom Auto Repair</strong>
        <br>100 1st street
        <br>Austin, TX 78704
        <br>PH:<a href="tel:(512)555-1212"">(512)555-1212</a> | Fax:(512)555-1212
        <br>Email:<a href="mailto:info@ourwebsite.com">info@ourwebsite.com</a>
</address>
</span>
```

The footers first span class has the name location and is defined in our CSS file. The location class tells the footer to position itself at the very bottom of the screen, to color the background, and to be a specific height and width. We will look at the CSS in a minute.

The next tag is the Address tag and is very important to both our first and second user. The Address tag tells our first user we are in a specific location and will help in making us more relevant to people searching for our products and services when they are close to us. The Address tag is also important to the second user because it tells them how to locate us should they want to do business with us. Even if your customers never come to you they still need to know you are local to them. As shown above your Address tag should at a minimum provide your company name, address, city, state, zip code, phone, fax, and email address.

Next is the copyright section.

```
<span class="copyright">&copy Copyright 2014 <a href="http://www.ourwebsite.com/">Custom Auto Repair</a></span>
```

We define the copyright class in the CSS file to provide positioning on the lower portion of the page. This section provides another opportunity to use our keyword phrase as the visible text in a link to our home page.

The last two section of our HTML document contain our navigation. As stated earlier although our navigation is displayed at the top of our web page, we design it lower in the HTML document and then use CSS to position it where we want it on our web page.

```
<ul id="navigation">
<li><a href="http://www.ourwebsite.com/AutoRepair/service">Schedule Service</a></li>
    <li><a href="http://www.ourwebsite.com/AutoRepair/quote">Request a Quote</a></li>
    <li><a href="http://www.ourwebsite.com/AutoRepair/schedule">Schedule Service</a></li>
    <li><a href="http://www.ourwebsite.com/AutoRepair/order">Order Parts</a></li>
    <li><a href="http://www.ourwebsite.com/AutoRepair/roadside">Roadside Assistance</a></li>
    <li><a href="http://www.ourwebsite.com/AutoRepair/contact">Contact Us</a></li>
  </ul>
```

One very important thing to keep in mind when creating links for your navigation is to always use fully qualified URLs and not just the directory and filename of the link. Above our links are fully qualified by using "http://www.ourwebsite.com/" and not just "/AutoRepair/folder name".

Another important thing to notice is the use of directories. Try to use directory names that match your content. You will notice above that our Schedule Service link is in the "AutoRepair/service" directory.

The last section of our HTML document befor we close the document is the breadcrumb section.

```
<ul id="breadcrumb">
  <li><a href="/Auto Repair/">Auto Repair</a></li>
  <li>></li>
  <li>Custom Auto Repair</li>
</ul>
```

The breadcrumb section is defined in the lower portion of our HTML document and uses CSS to position it where we want it to be displayed on our web page. Breadcrumbs allow our users to know where they are in the overall navigation of our website. Again we use this section to also provide another opportunity to use our keyword phrase on the page.

Let's take a quick look at the CSS file we created to position and format the web page. In this case we created a file named style.css. The CSS file is a standard text document with the .css extension.

```
#navigation {position:absolute; top:10px; left:450px; width:100%;}
#navigation li {display:inline;}

#breadcrumb {position:absolute; top:50px; left:50px; width:100%;}
#breadcrumb li {display: inline;}

#bodyDiv {position:absolute; top:150px; left:10px; width:90%; height:100%;}

.footer {position:absolute; left:0px; bottom:0; height:155px; width:100%; background-color:tan;}

.location {position:relative; top:10px; left:30px; }
.copyright {position:absolute; bottom:0; left:30%; }
```

The style.css file in this case is very simple with only a few lines of instructions. As we further develop our web page and our website we can continue to add more instructions to this file. Our first user "search engine bots" do not care about our CSS file or its contents, this file is used to provide positioning and formatting for our second user "the human user". As we further develop our website we would use the CSS file to create a rodust user friendly and great looking website.

Looking at the file contents above you should notice we have defined instructions in two different manors. The navigation, breadcrumb, and bodyDiv instructions have a leading # symbol that indicates we are referencing the ID of an element in our HTML document. An example from our code can be found by looking at the breadcrumb section. You will notice the <ul> Id is breadcrumb.

```
<ul id="breadcrumb">
  <li><a href="/Auto Repair/">Auto Repair</a></li>
  <li>></li>
  <li>Custom Auto Repair</li>
</ul>
```

We also provide instructions in the CSS file for the <li> elements by referencing the parent element followed by the child element we want to modify. ***#breadcrumb li { display: inline;}*** in this case we are telling the <li> element to position all the data in a horizontal line as apposed to a vertical list.

The instructions with a leading period like .footer define a class that can be used by any element that wishes to access that class. An example in our code is the footer section:

```
<div class="footer">
<span class ="location">
<address>
        <br><strong>Custom Auto Repair</strong>
        <br>100 1st street
        <br>Austin, TX 78704
        <br>PH:<a href="tel:(512)555-1212"">(512)555-1212</a| | Fax:(512)555-1212
        <br>Email:<a href="mailto:info@ourwebsite.com">info@ourwebsite.com</a>
</address>
</span>
```

The div element assigns the footer class from our CSS file to the element and any instructions in the footer class can be applied to the div.

From here we can take our web page and add more content, links to other web pages or websites, add a great UI to make the web page enjoyable and even add images, video, audio, a twitter or facebook feed, or a form to collect user data. The important point is we have a simple foundation that is a great start to getting search engines to notice we are very relevant in Austin, Tx for any users looking for Auto Repair.

There are many more SEO helpful tags and content points we can add to this page but for now we have developed a page we can use as a template for the rest of the website. It only will take a few graphics and a little CSS formatting to convert our SEO friendly HTML document into a professionally looking web page.

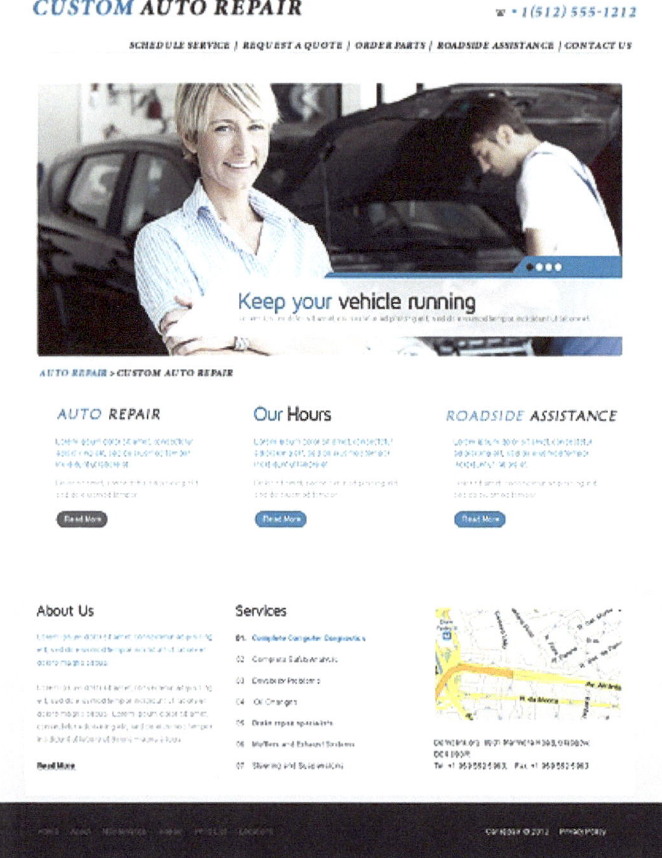

If you need further information on how to develop web pages and CSS files look on Google for solutions, there are great resources that can teach you how to make a great looking website. You can also purchase website templates and use what you have learned here to modify the html document to be SEO friendly. Search for “html templates” and you will find thousands of options available.

Content Is King

It holds true in any website national, or local, but specifically when your requirement is to capture a target audience in a specific geographical location. Chances are pretty good that there are other businesses in the same area with the same products or services. Maybe your better at what you do than they are, maybe your price is better. Let the target audience know what you have to offer by creating fresh content that informs them about your business and what it offers as well as why you're the better choice. Later in this book we will discuss creating content that converts website visitors to customers but for now let's take a look at where your content should be, and how often you should create new content.

To start with your web pages need content that speaks about your business, the product(s) or service(s), and has to include the targeted keyword phrases you need to capture for that page. The code example in the previous chapter involved creating a HTML document that would be used as a template for an auto repair shop. So following that example we would want to create content for our services page describing our services, what they are, why we are a better choice, how our rates are fair or better than the competition, and will include the keyword phrase we are targeting. Maybe for the page title we change it to be:

```
<title>Auto Repair | Oil Change | Tires | Brakes | Exhaust |
Custom Auto Repair Austin, TX</title>
```

We might change our Meta description to read:

```
<meta name="description" content="Custom Auto Repair of
Austin, TX offers complete automotive repair services for
all of your car care needs. We provide quality oil change,
brake and tire services from honest and local Austin, TX
```

```
professional technicians to restore your car to top
condition. Call today to schedule an appointment!"/>
```

Then we will add some content to the body of the page:

```
Custom Auto Repair is a certified NAPA AutoCare, family owned and operated,
auto service center serving Austin, Central Austin TX, and surrounding
areas. Since 1987, we have provided top-notch quality service. Our NAPA ASE
Tech of the Year award-winning mechanics are genuinely interested in
solving your auto repair issues and servicing your general automotive
maintenance! They are dedicated to delivering you complete satisfaction. In
fact, in a recent customer survey, we received 100% customer satisfaction!


Our ASE (Automotive Service Excellence) Certified Technicians are skilled
on all levels, from basic automotive maintenance such as an oil change and
state inspections to more complex car repair issues like brake repair,
Engine rebuilds, and transmission service. Our NAPA ASE Tech of the Year
award-winning mechanics have won the prestigious award 2 times and
counting!


At Custom Auto Repair, you'll never hear "Sorry, you're out of warranty."
We strive to ensure that everything we do raises the reputation of the
entire auto repair industry! We offer Austin's best Lifetime Warranty, as
well as free local shuttle service, free WiFi in our waiting area, free
a/c, alignment, trouble code, brake checks, and available financing!
```

This web page is now ready to capture a top spot on the Google search page for ***"Auto Repair"*** in Austin, TX.

Another way to generate great content is to add a blog to your website. By having a blog you can quickly fill two separate but very needs. You can create posts on topics that are about your industry, products, and services, and create how-to posts to inform your readers. This helps generate fresh new content every time you post. You can also quickly become known as an industry expert by providing valuable information.

So create great content that will set you apart from your competitors, include your keyword phrases, and be helpful and knowledgeable by posting and you will find your website well on its way to the top in your local market.

Adding Citations and directories

I have already mentioned the overwhelming importance in creating citations for your business website so let's create one. For this example we will create a citation on Yelp, the URL to access is https://biz.yelp.com/support . Once you access the yelp support page select the red ***"Create Your Free Account Now"*** button to get started.

Support Center

What Is Yelp?

Yelp aims to connect people with great local businesses and Yelp Business Accounts allow businesses to share information with the Yelp Community. Simply put, it's word of mouth -- amplified.

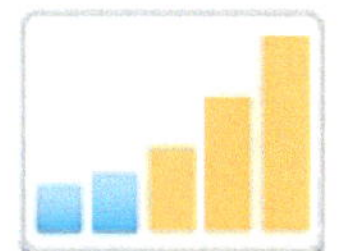

Create a Yelp Deal

Turn Yelp visitors into paying customers. Create a Deal in minutes. When Yelp users buy your Deal, you get paid.

Message Your Customers

You have a voice, so join the conversation regarding a business, reply to reviews either publicly or privately.

View Business Trends

What's word-of-mouth doing for you? Stats and charts measure the performance of a business page on Yelp.

Over 117 million people visited Yelp in Q3 2013 to make spending decisions. To help businesses get the most out of their online presence, Yelp Business Accounts offer a suite of FREE tools for businesses.

- Communicate with your customers-- privately and publicly
- Track how many people view your business page
- Add photos, a detailed business description, up-to-date information, history, and specialties
- Recommend other businesses

Create Your Free Account Now

On the next screen you may have another red button to select or you may go directly to the business owner's page. Once you are on the business owners page enter your business information to see if it is found.

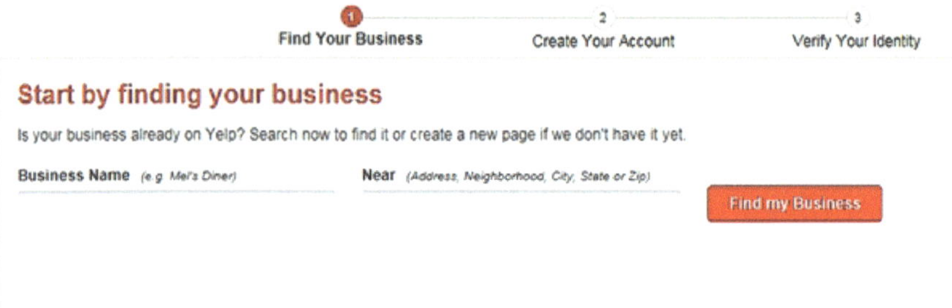

If you do not find your business already listed don't worry you can add it from a link at the bottom of the results on this page.

1 to 10 of 204 | Page: **1** 2 3 4 5 6 7 8 9 ...

Can't find your business? Add your business to Yelp

After you select the ***"Add your business"*** to Yelp link you will see the form you will use to enter your business information.

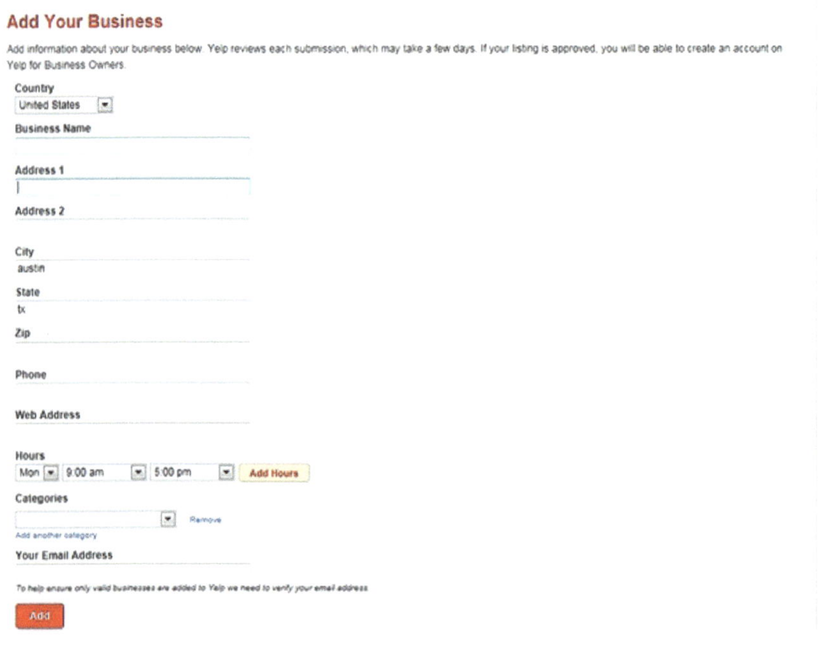

It is very important you provide all the correct information so this citation properly links to your business. After you have completed the form select the Add button. The last step is to Verify Your Identity. Yelp will present you with several options on ways you can verify your business identity.

Google places will be a very important listing for your business. Be sure to get your Google place listing as soon as possible as the verification process is a bit time consuming because they require you provide a physical address so they can mail you a verification card.

To claim your company's Google place visit http://www.google.com/+/business/ and select ***"Get your page"***

Get your business on Google for free

Your Google+ page connects you with customers, whether they're looking for you on Search, Maps, Google+ or mobile devices. Best of all, it's free. Really, we mean it.

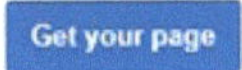

Next pick a category that best fits your business.

Local Business or Place
Hotels, restaurants, places, stores, services ...

Product or Brand
Apparel, cars, electronics, financial services ...

Company, Institution or Organization
Companies, organizations, institutions, non-profits ...

Arts, Entertainment or Sports
Movies, TV, music, books, sports, shows ...

Other
Use if your page doesn't fit in another category.

Enter your business name and address and fill in the rest of your business information. Answer all the questions with correct information and ensure it matches the information you entered on the yelp website as well as any other citation or directory websites you use.

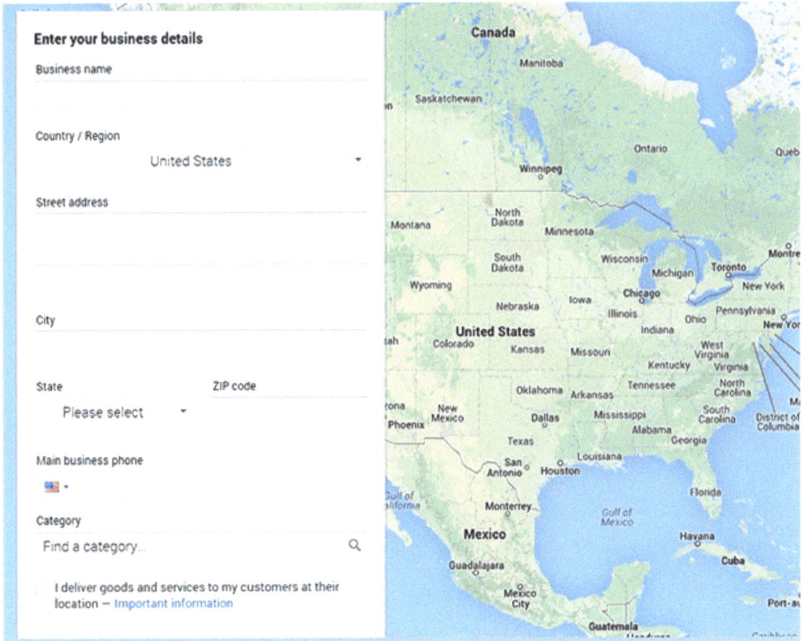

Once complete you will be presented with a screen informing you that Google will send you a verification card within 1-2 weeks.

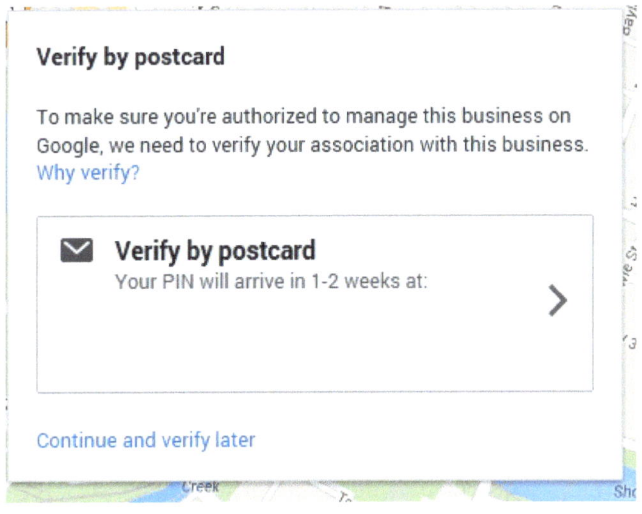

Ensure the address that Google is sending your postcard to is the correct address for your business mail. This will also be the address Google Maps uses to display your business on the Google search engine response page.

Most Citation and directory site are similar in the methods and requirements for creating an account. I cannot stress enough the importance of taking your time and ensuring the information you provide is correct.

Continue to add new citations and directories as often as you can. The more external points you have pointing back to your website the more your business website will benefit.

Be sure to create a Facebook, Twitter and LinkedIn profile as well and be as active as time allows. Try to post at least ones a week on each platform but mix it up and don't simply copy and paste content. It is a good idea to use the social network platforms to make customers and potential customers aware of special offers you have on your products and services. I recommend you create some deals specific to customers who contact you from one of these platforms.

If you purchase supplies from a local supplier contact them about doing a link exchange, you will put a link to their website on your business site and they will do the same for you. This is sometimes the easiest way to develop quality links for your website.

Building User Reviews

Now that you have developed a website that is properly SEO formatted and you have started down the road of developing powerful links thru citations, directories, and suppliers, it's time to get your customers involved in a two way conversation.

I say two way conversation because many businesses fail in understanding that that is what a review really is. It is a customer telling you "the business" in a very public forum what they thought about doing business with you and if your product or service was worth the cost.

A lot of businesses don't realize that a customer is 85% more likely to write a bad review in the heat of the moment than they are to take the time to write a good review for service that was just ok, and customers that absolutely loved your product or service will write a positive review only 17% of the time. To get the percentages of positive reviews up for your business you have to be diligent in asking your customers to take a few minutes and write the review. Don't be afraid to ask for a review and don't be afraid to offer rewards to customers willing to write reviews. But beyond everything else NEVER, NEVER, NEVER write a false review.

Be sure to stay on top of the reviews your business gets and always respond to negative reviews with an offer to make it better. If a customer writes a review saying service was poor, or the product was defective, respond to the review with an offer to provide the service again at no cost, or replace the product. It isn't a bad thing if a business has a bad day, but it is a bad thing not to fit it. Potential customers reading the review will be much more likely to take a chance with you if they see you are willing to correct any issues that may arise.

You should have the website addresses of several citation sites printed on cards you can hand out to customers to remind them to create reviews. The easier you can make it on your customers to provide a positive review the more reviews you will have. Let's face it if you search for a restaurant to eat at and you find two you think you would like but one of them has bad reviews and the other one has great reviews, you will be eating the one with great reviews.

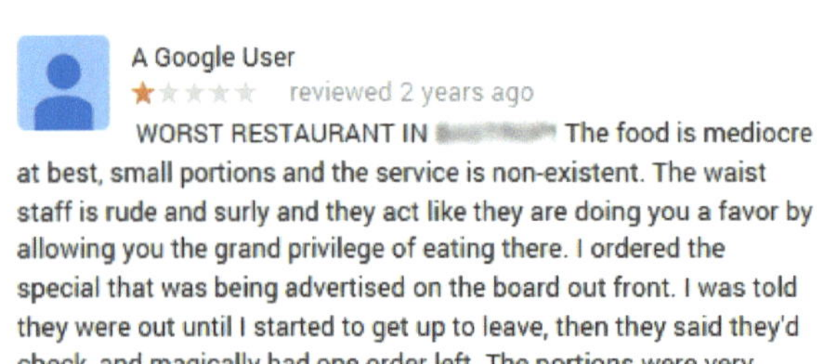
A Google User
reviewed 2 years ago
WORST RESTAURANT IN The food is mediocre at best, small portions and the service is non-existent. The waist staff is rude and surly and they act like they are doing you a favor by allowing you the grand privilege of eating there. I ordered the special that was being advertised on the board out front. I was told they were out until I started to get up to leave, then they said they'd check, and maqically had one order left. The portions were very
...
Liked: Atmosphere
Disliked: Food, Service, Value

Let's face it, it is impossible to please everyone all the time but as a business owner you really have to do your best and when your best just isn't good enough for someone ask them *"what can I do to make you a happy customer?"* you will be surprised how many people are willing to tell you exactly what you need to do to please them and many are happier with the fact you made an effort.

Measuring Website Results

The way we define the local marketplace has changed with the use of websites and local search and now we as business owners have to understand how to measure what is working and what is not.

It used to be you could simply place a sign in front of your business and if customers walked in you knew it worked. Then you could place an advertisement in the paper or run an ad on the radio and if business spiked you knew it had a positive impact.

With a website you have multiple pages and entry points and you need to know what pages get visits, how long they stay on the page, if they click on a link on the page, or hit the back button and bounce back to the search engine. Without any method in place to measure the success of a web page you don't know if it is worth the cost and time to continue to work on it.

Let's say you have a web page in your business website and it offers a free oil change with the purchase of a tune-up. A customer comes into your business and asks for a tune-up, do they get a free oil change because they visited your web page or did they just happen to see the sign out front that says you do tune-ups for a low cost?

Maybe walk-in customers pay $99.00 for a tune-up without the free oil change and website visitors pay $89.99 and get a free oil change. If you don't know how the customer arrived at the decission to do business with you than what do you charge them and what services do they get?

You need to ensure you know how customers arrived to the decision to do business with you so you have an idea of where to spend your valuable time developing your website and business.

What Tools to Use

Measuring Website Results is an important component in developing a successful business online, it tells you where visitors come from, what they did while on your web page, how long they stayed, and much more. Once you have this information you can make decisions about how to create new pages that will bring even more business to your website. This is also the building block for directing targeted traffic to your site and converting that traffic into paying customers (covered later in this book).

A great and free tool to use is Google Analytics -

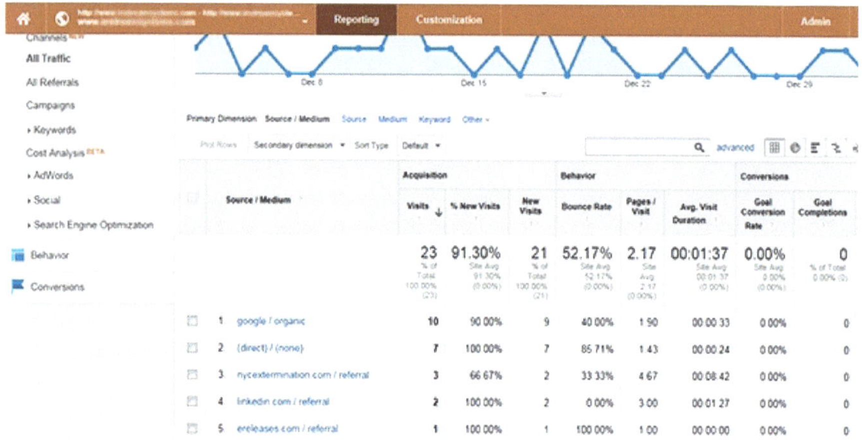

To get started measuring your business results; navigate to http://www.google.com/analytics/ and login using the userId and password you created for your Google places account. If you do not have a Google user account yet create one.

Once logged in, set up your website to use the Google analytics. Fill out the form completely ensuring all elements you want to track are included. You will need to provide your website address (URL) as well.

What would you like to track?

Website	Mobile app

Select a tracking method

Use Classic Analytics if you want to use the *dc.js* JavaScript or any related features, including Remarketing, Google Display Network Integration, DoubleClick for Advertisers Integration, or DoubleClick Search Integration.

Features	Universal Analytics BETA	Classic Analytics
Basic GA features (Visitor acquisition, behavior, and conversion data)	✓	✓
Event tracking	✓	✓
AdWords account linking	✓	✓
Custom variables	Upgrade to custom dimensions & metrics	✓
Custom dimensions & metrics	✓	
Online/offline data sync	✓	
Multi-platform tracking	✓	
Simplified configuration controls	✓	
Select new feature releases	✓	
Advanced advertisement tools (DFA, Remarketing)	Coming soon	✓

To use Universal Analytics, implement the new tracking code snippet you'll see at the end of this sign-up process.

Setting up your account

Account Name

After the form is completed you will select the ***"Get Tracking ID"*** button at the bottom of the page. The Tracking ID identifies your website to your Google Analytics account

Navigate to your Google Analytics home page located at: https://www.google.com/analytics and select the "Admin" button at the top right of the screen. Then select "Tracking Info from the center of the screen.

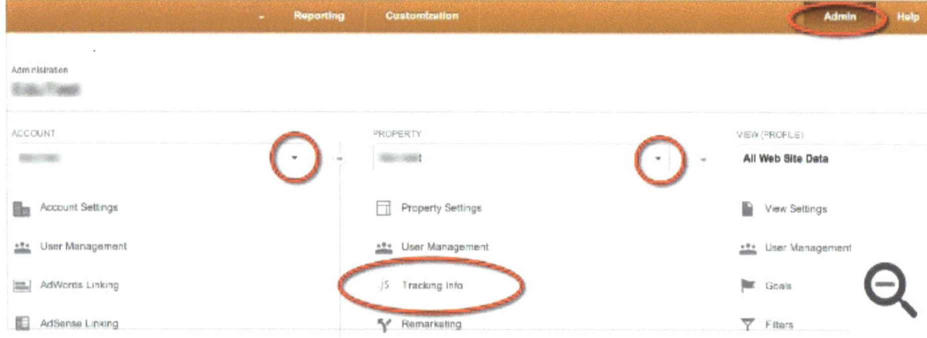

To access the HTML and Javascript code you will need to enable tracking on your website, scroll to the bottom of the page as shown below.

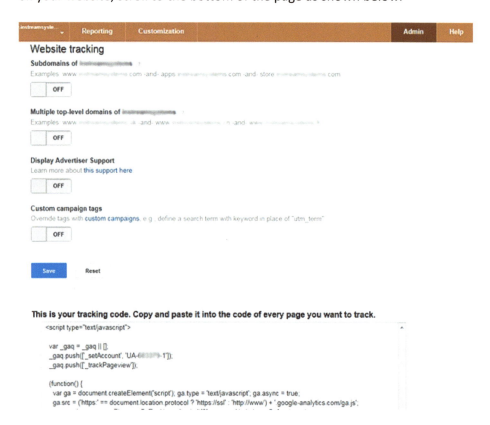

Reporting Customization Admin Help

Website tracking

Subdomains of

Examples: www. .com -and- apps. .com -and- store. .com

OFF

Multiple top-level domains of

Examples: www. -and- www. -and- www.

OFF

Display Advertiser Support

Learn more about this support here

OFF

Custom campaign tags

Override tags with custom campaigns, e.g., define a search term with keyword in place of "utm_term"

OFF

Save Reset

This is your tracking code. Copy and paste it into the code of every page you want to track.

```
<script type="text/javascript">

  var _gaq = _gaq || [];
  _gaq.push(['_setAccount', 'UA-[illegible]-1']);
  _gaq.push(['_trackPageview']);

  (function() {
    var ga = document.createElement('script'); ga.type = 'text/javascript'; ga.async = true;
    ga.src = ('https:' == document.location.protocol ? 'https://ssl' : 'http://www') + '.google-analytics.com/ga.js';
```

Copy and paste the code into the header section of your HTML document on each web page you build for your website. Once Google starts gathering data from visitors to your website you will know how customers got to your website and what keywords got them there to name just a few reported pieces of data.

Keep It Simple Stupid

Google Analytics can be very robust or very easy it depends on your needs and the amount of time you want to dedicate to setting it up and becoming familiar with all it has to offer. My recommendation to start with is to set it up as shown above and monitor the built-in reporting available until it no longer fills your needs. The goal here is to provide you with a tool to help validate you are doing the right things and not to take on another time consuming job.

For more in-depth information on using Google analytics search for Google Analytics tutorial and you will find websites, videos, and books that are very detailed in this topic. For now you have enough information to get Google Analytics up and running.

Making Adjustments

Your business website is up and running and you can now be found online thru a local Google search, but to be honest the work is just now starting. Maybe you have captured one of the ten available organic spots on the result page for your keyword phrase, there is much more you can do. For every keyword phrase you should try to capture several of the first page positions and you can do this by following what you have learned throughout this book.

One of the best ways to capture multiple spots on a result page is thru the use of your web page with relevant content, the local business section with Google Maps, and the use of video.

You have a very strong service page on your website, so let's also create a video introducing your certified technicians and showing what your service bay's look like. You don't need any special tools to create a good video to post on YouTube, you're smart phone will do just fine. The website huffingtonpost.com has a great article on just how to do it:

http://www.huffingtonpost.com/britt-michaelian/how-to-create-professiona_b_3062287.html

In the chapter "How to Get Citations and Backlinks" we walked thru setting up our account for Google Places. Now we need to get past and current customers to write positive reviews on our Google plus page. Positive reviews are not only a decision point for potential customers but are used in Google algorithm to position you on result pages.

You will need to continue to develop your business website by creating new pages that take advantage new keyword phrases to positing you on more and more response pages in the search engines. Try to break down your products and services to one per page. An example would be to create a page specific to break replacement, or termite control & treatment. By breaking down your products and services to one per page you create the ability to capture the local market for keyword phrases specific to that individual product or service.

What Next

I could have mentioned this earlier in this book but I really wanted to focus on it here in this chapter, after you have already successfully developed your website and have it listed on Google. I always find it valuable to look at the websites of my local competitors that rank higher in search results than I do to see why they are seen by Google as more relevant.

One of the reasons I like to wait until after development to do this is so my focus on the business I am developing for doesn't get clouded by the content provided by competitors. For example if my competitor states We are Austin's' only 4-person certified team, I do not want to get stuck on that and try to outdo them by stating we are Austin's only 5-person certified team. That verbiage is just too close to the competitor's content and it would be taken by anyone reading both websites in a bad way.

Instead I rather develop the website and get listed and then compare to see where we can improve. Most often you will find subtle changes you can make in order to improve your position. For example say the competitor's website has a listing of other auto repair shops in the area and the hourly rate differences. Most often their hourly rate will be slightly lower.

Our website may show a graph of how much faster we get the job done compared to the average time of other service centers. This approach provides us a great set of content, shows we do great work in a timely manor, and takes hourly cost out of the equation due to it taking less time overall.

Read your competitors websites, compare but do not copy, and come up with content ideas to separate the competition from your company. I am sure I do not need to say this but just in case, *"Never Talk Bad About Your Competition"* it really comes off in a negative way.

The reality is when done correctly you never finish SEO it really is a constant job, however once up and running your required time can be as little as 5-hours a week. If you learn to dedicate a few minutes each morning to posting on your social profiles, and spend 3-4 hours a week writing an article for your blog, and spend a few minutes reviewing your Google Analytics reports, and an hour or so reviewing your competition you can really see it payoff quickly.

Even if you end up hiring a company or an individual to take over the SEO responsibility for you I recommend you stay as active as you can to ensure your cost of that hire is getting you the results you need.

Bonus Chapter: Protecting Your Business Online Reputation

Protecting your reputation online for a business is mostly about responding to negative reviews if you ever get one. One of the best things to do is respond immediately to a negative review and offer a solution, do not just say sorry, or try to make excuses for poor products or services.

This is also another reason positive reviews are so important. If you do get a negative review and respond to it a lot of positive reviews can quickly burry it as well as put a positive feeling about doing business with you.

Another very important aspect of protecting your reputation is to ensure you have claimed ownership of your brand. Make sure you have a Facebook page in your business name, a Twitter account in your business name, a Google Places page, Yelp, Yellow Pages, and so on.

Don't allow someone else to open a social account in your business it is too easy for them to make your business you look bad. You would be surprise how often this has happened.

If you find that someone has opened a social account in your business name contact the holders of that social network and ask them to remove the account or require the owner of the account to change their name on the account.

As long as your business name is registered most all social networks will be happy to assist you in protecting your brand name. you can write a simple letter or email to them, something like the following should do the job.

[Dear Sir or Madam,

*As the registered holder of the brand name **"Your business name"** I am writing you today to get your assistance in putting a stop to some reputation damaging content being published by a user of your network. The account **"profile name"** has posted several items that are being confused with the thoughts and position of my business and it is my belief has already caused damage to my brand. Due to the profile name being the same as a registered business name I am requesting you remove the account or require the holder of the profile to change the name associated with the account. Your assistance in this matter in a timely manor is very much appreciated.*

For any questions or follow up please contact me using the information provided in the signature line of this document.

Sincerely,

You're Name, Business name

Address, city, st , zip code

Phone number

Fax number

Email address

Your signature line

Date of letter or email]

I cannot guarantee you a response however most of the social networks I have contacted in this way over the past few years have been more than helpful. You can also contact the holder of the profile and make let them know you are aware of the profile and by using your business name on the social network they may be causing reputation issues for your business. Be very polite with them and you will have a much better chance to get them to comply.

If you previously worked with an SEO company and they setup any social network profiles in your business name and you are having issues getting them to turn over ownership of the profiles, contact their office and inform them you intend to protect your business brand at all cost and would like to provide them an opportunity to resolve the issue quietly first. Most of the companies do not want to have bad press and will work with you. Again you can be firm but be polite.

Bonus Chapter: How to convert visitors into customers

This single chapter is more than worth the price of this book. The ability to convert site visitors into paying customers is the holy grail of any online business. It doesn't matter if you sell your products online and never meet your customers, or if you get new customers from your website and then fulfill your customers needs in person.

When a visitor clicks a link from a search engine and lands on one of your web pages you have 5-9 seconds to convince them you have what they are looking for. How you do that is by providing them information about your product or service, answer their questions without them having to ask them, and providing them a method of acting on that information.

The starting point is getting visitors to convert from someone just looking around your website, to someone who takes action and orders, calls, or clicks on a request for more info link. The first thing you have to do is get their buy in on what you offer.

Interesting enough it isn't that you have the best price, or the best product. Often you also have to understand what makes a person desire to be a part of what you offer. You really need to understand what makes people act, believe me the big guy's in marketing have had this covered for many years.

To convert website visitors into paying customers you have to master the process of the nudge. There are hundreds of books, websites, and white papers that cover the topic of how to convert but it really all boils down to understanding how to gently guide your visitor to a specific point.

One way to convert is to use cues. A cue can be text or a graphic. For example let's say a small antique shop wants to lower their energy cost. They noticed many customers enter their front door and don't close the door all the way so they put a small sign on their door asking customers to help them save the planet by reducing the energy used to run the air conditioner and all the customer needs to do is please close the door behind them. You would be amazed how many customers close the door and feel good about it.

How can you use the concept of "nudging" to convert visitors into paying customers? Firstly, think about all the information that potential buyers need to make a decision to buy from you and put that information on your webpage. Then, answer the types of questions that you or your customer service team frequently answers on the phone, on the web page. In addition, make it easy to find this information. Lastly, don't let your site visitors get lost looking for how to contact you. With these simple "nudges" you can turn your website visitors into buyers.

Call-to-Action is another tool used to convert visitors into paying customers. How many times have you made a sale without asking your customer to buy? Think about it, you get a call or some form of request to fulfill a service. You look at what it will take to complete the service and you provide a cost, next you ask "So do you want me to get started?" that is a call-to-action. On your web page you need to ask for the sale and there are many ways you can do this in a successful way.

When you're creating your first call-to-action, it's easy to end up making something that people won't click on. To save you time and effort, here are the essential elements of a quality call-to-action.

- **Eye-Catching Design:** For someone to click on your call-to-action, they have to first notice it. Your colors should contrast with your website design to enable the image to stand out on the page, yet also appear large enough to be noticed (I've seen them perform best around 225px wide and 45px high).

- **Content That Makes People Want to Act:** It's not enough to say "Submit" as your call-to-action content -- you need a concise, jargon-free phrase that uses actionable verbs to catch people's attention.

- **Clear Value:** Visitors should know exactly what will happen when they click on a call-to-action. Are they expecting to Get a free service quote, or See a list of prices? Make sure the call-to-action explicitly tells them what they're getting in exchange for their click.

- **A Specific Page (Ideally a Landing Page) Aligned With One Stage in the Sales Cycle:** A call-to-action is *most effective* if people are taken to a dedicated landing page after clicking it, rather than a random page on your website. For example, a call-to-action is still a call-to-action if it points to a "contact us" page (which isn't a landing page), but it won't be as effective driving leads and customers as a specific, focused landing page for a free estimate. Also, a call-to-action should be created with a specific stage in the sales cycle in mind.

To create a great call-to-action you need to follow the rules of writing ad copy. Start sentences with subjects and verbs. Verbs and subjects help us to quickly glean the meaning of a sentence and that's important when you only have seconds to get your site visitors attention.

We also need emotional triggers that forge a bond or elicit a positive feeling from our visitors. Everyone wants to be in the in-crowd, so you should try to write a call-to-action that says something like "70% of our customers choose this option".

Look at the below call-to-action, it does several things right.

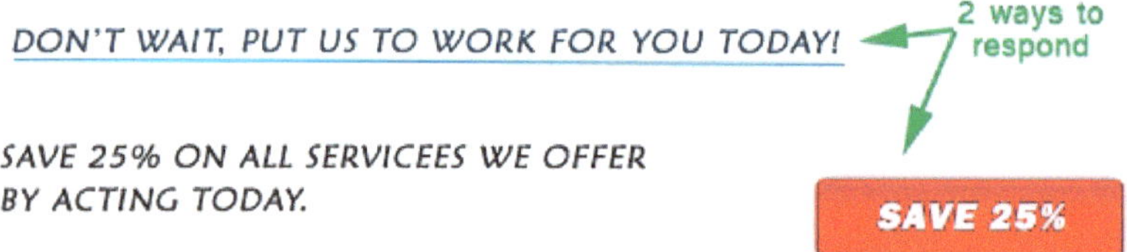

First it provides 2 ways for the user to respond. The text "Don't Wait, put us to work for you today" is a hyperlink the user can click on, and the red "Save 25%" button. Also it implies no work on the visitor's part. It's completely benefits-oriented and personal, asking you to put Us to work... for you.

There isn't a vague, uninspiring "click here" command. The link is embedded in the benefit statement. And that statement is phrased as a command, so visitors can't miss it.

Use your imagination when creating your call-to-action and be sure you provide a benefit to the visitor for clicking on it. Make sure the call-to-action informs the visitor what to expect when they select it. In the above it is clear the user will save 25% off the cost of services by clicking on the call-to-action.

Your take away from this chapter are simple; provide your visitors with the information, answer the questions, ask for the sale while providing a compelling reason they should choose you, let them know what they will get, provide simple access to contact you.

Index

www.ingramcontent.com/pod-product-compliance
Lightning Source LLC
Chambersburg PA
CBHW041144050326
40689CB00001B/478